D1262863

Other Books by Michael Robinson

Freedom of Silence
The Earth and the Dancing Man
Touching the Serpent's Tail

A Bird Within a Ring of Fire

by

Michael Robinson

Second impression

Text copyright   1998 Michael Robinson
Text illustrations   1998 Michael Robinson

All rights reserved. No part of this publication may be
reproduced, stored in a retrieval system, or
transmitted in any form or by any means, electronic,
mechanical, photocopying, recording, or
otherwise, without the prior written permission of Martin
House, R.R. #1, Keene, Ontario, Canada, K0L 2G0.
(705)295-4491, fax (705)295-4124.

Printed in Canada by The Vincent Press Ltd.

Canadian Cataloguing in Publication Data

Robinson, Michael, 1948 -
A Bird Within a Ring of Fire
ISBN No 0-9695225-3-3

1. Indians of North America - Poetry. 1. Title
PS8585.035173B57 1998a C811'.54 C98-900824-X
PR9199.3.R536B57 1998a

Martin House Publishing,
R.R.#1, Keene, Ontario K0L 2G0
(705)295-4491   fax (705)295-4124

Dedicated to the memory of

Mary Lou Fox Radulovich
Ode Min Kwe

A gentle heart
whose fire
lights up the stars

The Illustrations

The Poems

We started as Birds
with the wisdom of Birds,
But we sold our
wings
for Gold.

Authors Note:

My writings and my images explore a lost History[1]
and a uncertain future of the natural world
and man's place and responsibility within this living
History. My point of reference is the Earth[2]. It is
through Her eyes, Her perception of reality, that I
watch the world go by. It is through this
commitment of clarity[3] that I have learned not to
judge History as a single study but to understand
that there is a past, present and future to History.
These are Time Posts that mark the passing of time
in parallel with seasons and mankinds responses to
these ever moving, ever changing points of view,
whether they are in conflict, harmony or apathy.

My work is much like History. It must stand on
its own and be judged on its own merit, allowing
the viewer or traveler to choose their own meaning
or response.

I dreamed in the dream time
and dreamed in the real time
but my sleep is kept
in a secret place,
protected from the stars
and the birds[4] of the night.

My words are carefully chosen
for fear of having to repeat them
or someone misusing them.
Somewhere in the black of space,
beyond the moon
a part of me waits
alone
with the cold
and the indifference
of a stranger.

Seeing Fire For the First Time

Seeing Fire For the First Time

A tiny bird
in a ring of fire.
A ring within a ring
of fire.

A ring of Ghosts[5]
surround the bird,
moving slowly
in a circle.
Never tiring.
Chanting ancient
bird-like chants.

A cool wind
that was passing by,
whispered in the bird's ear;
a battle cry,
offering the bird
a chance to leave.
But the bird whispered back
"Here, I'm free.
I'm learning
to be invisible
in a world
of Ghosts."

Freedom Road

I suddenly realized there was a man
sitting on the ground
between the buildings I was passing.
He was grinning at me.
Then to my horror
I noticed that he was chained
to the ground.
"My name is freedom[6]." he suddenly said loudly.
"You like my chain?" He giggled,
holding up his leg.
"You know, no one really wants
to be free.
You think you do, though."
His voice was suddenly cold.
"Come on now, be true,
You are looking for freedom!
I can smell it."
He leaned forward and began sniffing
the air.
His face quickly broke out
in a comical grin.
He began to laugh.
"Actually I did know a man
who was free,
but he was invisible."
He fell back laughing again.
I turned and left the village
as fast as I could,
as he yelled after me,
"Wait, I also knew a man
who spent his entire life
looking for freedom.
He even wrote a song about it.
Listen!
Listen!

I'll sing it for you!"
I broke into a run
as though death itself
was right behind me.
Suddenly I froze in mid-stride.
I couldn't move,
couldn't breathe.
It felt as though my whole body
was being slowly crushed...
pulled down on to the spot
where I stood.
Then I heard the chain...
I could hear it racing up behind me!
My fear was so intense,
I felt I was going to explode.
I could hear the chain rattling
and hissing like a snake,
I knew it was death!
"No, the chain is not death!",
the crazy man yelled.
God, he too, was right behind me.
No, he was high above my head;
yelling and twisting in the mad circles
among the tree tops.
"The chain is freedom,
fabulous freedom, glorious freedom!"
Suddenly, he was standing
in front of me,
breathing in loud gasps.
"Would you like to buy my chain?"
He giggled, holding the chain
out, close to my face.
"Come on, buy it, it's not as
expensive as you think.

How much you got?
What's wrong, can't you speak?"
My mind was blank
with horror.
I could only stare at the chain.
It seemed alive.
His smile disappeared
and his eyes left my face
and began looking around my feet.
"You think this is the path
to freedom, don't you?
Well it's not!" His eyes
were cold as steel.
"It's just another path to another village.
But it is called the freedom road.
It goes that way
and that way." He pointed behind me
and in front.
His face softened, as he started to smile again.
"Actually, you probably think I am
making all this up.
I think that's it. You wouldn't know
freedom if it gave you something for
free," he giggled.
"Actually", he continued "I wouldn't sell
you my chain. It's mine."
He looked at the chain lovingly then
back at me.
He laughed again, but the laughter
was old. His eyes never leaving mine.
"I heard the questions you were asking
the old men in the village.
You know why your questions didn't
work?

They didn't know what you were
talking about.
Boy, were you ever stupid!
I bet you can't even remember
what they were.
I'll bet you my chain."
He suddenly broke up laughing,
then dropped the chain.
The metallic thud was like a snap,
releasing me from his invisible grip.
I quickly stepped back, as the man
suddenly lurched at me'
his arm outstretched.
I screamed and fell backwards,
sprawling hard on the ground.
Before I could do or say anything
he was gone,
vanished!

I slowly pulled myself up on my knees,
quickly looking all around.
The chain too, was gone.
I did not move for a long time,
partly out of fear that
any sudden movement
would bring the strange man back.
Then I heard him again, far away, singing.
I quickly stood up, facing
towards the village.
I could hear him yelling,
calling out to me.
"Don't worry'" he sang out,
"I can't hurt you.
I'm chained to the ground."

The Bird and the Poet

The Bear came to me
where I was hungry
and shared his food.
The Deer came to me
when I was lost
and showed me the way home.
The Wolf came to me
so I could sleep without fear.
The Turtle came to me
so I could fly across
the river of time....
The Crow came
and entered my body
through my eyes.

I said to the Bird
"You are trapped now
in the confines of my body"
"No," said the Crow
" I can now fly forever.
So far away that I will
disappear
even from your memory."

The Path of No Choice

The path went far into the future,
rolling up and down
like an endless
moving river.
Sparkling,
like the back of a silver snake,
with no head or tail.
And like a snake
it had a hypnotic beauty
camouflaging its true identity.

The Path of No Choice

I was on this path.
I had been travelling it
for a very long time.
I could not remember how long
or why?
Where I came from
or where I was going?
This was the path of no choices
but what I feared
more than being lost in time,
was being devoured by a snake.

The path went far into the future
rolling up and down
like an endless
moving river
and like the moving river,
a ghost like silver line
ran from the back of my head,
stretching far
behind me,
above the path.

It held on to me like a leash.
At times it pulled me back.
Then it would let me
run free.
I did not know
whether I was the pet
or the master?
Was I a boat,
floating on this river of time
or a child?
Was I lost
or was I leaving?
Was I a man, alive
or dead...
or was I the dreaded snake?
Could I make a choice
On the path of no choices?

The path went far into the future
and I went with it.

The Earth does not deal
with truth or logic.
The Earth deals with
the intent of truth
and movement.

The Eyes of a Bird

The Eyes
of a Bird

The temptation of reason
became a statement of tradition.
A last chance to listen.
It came as a song
in the middle of the night,
whispering,
over and over again,
that it was cold
and hungry.

Temptation sat huddled,
like a dejected child,
by our dwindling fire.
Waiting for salvation.
Waiting for dawn
and the black of night
to creep away
like a thief.

We said nothing,
so it stayed.

A Fire in the Sky

A Fire in the Sky

It is understood there is no right
or wrong.
There is no position or claim
of winning,
only degrees of losing,
of learning...,
Of replacing one thing for another.
It is understood and taught
that the only principal goal
of Man is 'choice'.
To understand the idea of choice
is to see the world
through the window
known as clarity
and then pass though.

Duality

The danger of any one reality
is that it is guarded
on both sides
by non-realities.
It is held in one place,
unable to move.
A prisoner.

Duality

The Earth gently moved
Her hand
so men could see Her.
She gave them
a gift;
a chance to be free.
She gave "Duality,"

This was Her last prayer
to the world of Men,
as She disappeared
into the night.
This was the last struggle
between a dream
and a song.
The last chance to listen
and dance
with silence.

She knew 'fear'
had entered the world,
blinding
and distorting men's view
of themselves
and of Her.

For the first time
in Her life,
She felt like a prisoner.

The Last World of Robert Moses

The Last World of Robert Moses

*I looked up
and saw a man
floating in the sky.
He was silver white.
I thought it was God.
I felt clean,
free.*

*As the sun set,
I looked again,
but the man floating
in the sky
was now dark
and empty.
It was me,
me.*

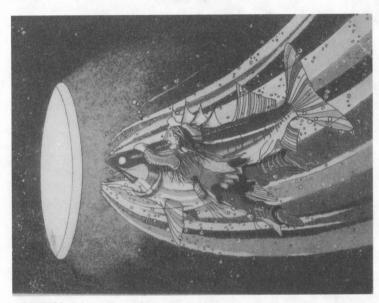

The Fifth River Running

The Fifth River Running

The Serpents[8] come to you
as groping hands,
reaching out
in the night
to tap your soul,
in an attempt to lure
your spirit
into the running river.

You wait a lifetime
to escape this dream.
To ease your fear.
But nights come and go
in the blink of an eye.
You soon
lose your way,
forgetting your real purpose
and drift away.
into someone else's
reality.

Millennium

Millennium

Our technology has long ago
out distanced our humanity,
continually widening
the gap between
the human spirit
and the natural world.

The natural world never stops.
Never waits,
for the sick or dying.
Man has failed to learn
that we stand in the earth's moving shadow
not the Earth standing in our frozen time.

We have created a system of time
that has created its own History.
We claim that History to be our own.
Now we stand facing
the end of the fourth civilization[9].
(Each block of time is represented by the moth or
    the gatekeeper.)
We now stand in the shadow
of not only an alien History
but in the shadow
of our own image.
We quickly looked back
for reassurance.
We see only black
We look forward
beyond our vanity
and see only our fear.

Millennium is a word
we created.
It is a time and a History
we thought was ours,
only to discover that it is not.

We are very much alone
in the universe.

25

Living in the Eagles Time

Living in the Eagles Time

We have been called angels.
We have been called witches.
We have been called priests
and children with the souls of birds.
Sometimes when we travel,
we never speak.
At night, we have disappeared
and returned as old singers.
We have been fire.
We have been smoke[10].

But today...
We are alone,
as we watch an angry lake
from a high rocky cliff.

The Responsibility of Knowledge

The Responsibility of Knowledge

My dream was one of fantasy
with no purpose
or fear.
I raced from one idea
to another,
passing over strange landscapes,
never having to stop
and became involved.
I neither took or gave.
It was a journey of pure pleasure.
My beliefs and my history
were left behind.
I felt no obligation to them
or that I had to bring them
or explain why I left them behind.

But when I awoke,
I was surprised how empty I felt.
Something was missing...
I slowly looked behind me,
as though I could look
back into my dream.
I saw no light
or silver clouds.

Only a dark tunnel
stared back at me,
cold, stone-like.
Suddenly I saw something
moving.

It was rolling,
slowly, side to side,
deep in the black hole.
To my horror,
I watched
as this alien figure
tried desperately
to pull itself along,
only to continuously slide back.
Its face, its pain;
It stared right at me
freezing my very soul.

I tore myself from my bed
and raced outside,
hoping my nightmare
would not follow me.

The Sun was bright
and warm
and quickly calmed my racing heart.
I slowly walked away
from the house...
Just to walk.

A large bird
flew over my field,
passing over my head
and my eyes followed its shadow
across the grass.

I stopped!
My eyes stared at the ground,
at my feet.
I slowly looked behind me,
then my right side,
my left side.
I looked at a small tree
in front of me.
Its shadow was strong.

I looked back at my feet.
I had no shadow!
Then slowly I looked behind me, at the house...,
* back at my dream.*

The Man Who Dreamed He Was Smoke

The Man Who Dreamed He Was Smoke

"Look at the rocks!
What do you see?" the old man said.
I see rocks." the boy replied
without hesitation.
"No, look again. What do you see?"
" I see... rocks" the boy answered slowly.
"Is this a game?" he continued.
"What am I suppose to see?"
When the old man did not answer,
the young boy looked up at him.
"Wait! I see lichens.
Is that it?... Lichens and stuff.
Is that what you see?"
"No." Said the man.
"When I look I see shadows.
I see fire.
Thousands of little fires.
I see birds with dark eyes.
Birds with white shadows.
I see tiny men
watching me.
I see them passing through
little holes in the rocks
coming and going.
I see an ancient face in the rocks.
Her eyes are closed.
Listen, you can hear her singing."
"I don't understand." The boy whispered.,
quickly becoming a bit concerned
at the old man's sanity.
"I don't see anything but rocks
and lichen." He whispered again.
The man seemed not to hear.

"If you listen," he put his hand to his ear.
"You can hear Her."
The young boy slowly looked back
at the rocks.
"What does she say?"
The man turned to the boy.
" 'I can give you no more time.'
That's what She says"
The old man turned back
to face the rocks.
"I remember when I was a boy"
he said quietly,'
"An old fellow told me
what he heard."
"What did he hear?" asked the boy.
The man closed his eyes
and answered.
"The rocks told the fellow
to run."

I heard the song
in the middle of the night,
long, long ago.
It came out of the Blackness
like a Ghost.
Whispering over and over again.
Strange words
in dark rhymes.
I heard no other cries
in the night.
So I took them.

Michipeshu Looking for Ghosts

Michipeshu Looking for Ghosts

I told the stranger
not to cross the Lake.
I knew that in a very short time
the Lake would be too rough
and not allow anyone to pass.
He smiled a big smile
and touched my arm,
inviting me
to return to my fire.
In a loud voice,
he announced
it was time to leave,
as he led
his family down to their boats.
With great ceremony
and laughter,
they left.
They were never seen again.

I told the man in black
to wait till morning,
to leave for the next village.
The trail was dark,
twisting,
with many rocks and holes.
He patted my arm
as though I was a child.
"God will show me the way"
he said with great conviction.
Then he left.
He was never seen again.

I touched the blindman's arm
and asked if I could help.
He jumped back
as though my hand
burned his arm.
In a loud voice
he told me
that even though he was blind,
he could see
more than me.
He then lifted his head
and sniffed the air.
"You smell", he added,
"besides I do not want
to go anywhere!"
He lay down and went to sleep.
I noticed that was all
he ever did.

The clarity of man's perception
of his life
is a fragile movement of shadows
and silence.
A strange little dance
through a long dark night.

The Looker

The Looker

We offered him warmth
but he waits
at the edge of night.
He chooses the dark
to warm his heart.
He was content
to sell his dreams
for the promise of gold
and as the waters of time
rose
He sank under the weight
of his greed.

The Watcher

The Watcher

Grey shadows criss-cross
his beating heart
as he sits huddled by his meagre fire,
suffering the injustices of cold
and growing old.

With one eye on the fire
and one eye on the horizon line,
the Hunter slowly releases
his shadow
from the bondage of his life.
Without promise or profit,
he sets his last memory
as a man,
free,
to wander forever
in the smoke above his fire.

Seer

Seer

Inside of me
flows a river
running deep and fast
on a journey
into the black mystery of night

In the river
huge fish
change into birds
then back into fish
at each beat of my heart

I now wait
shivering in the cold.
Soon I will become so small
that the smallest breeze
will blow me away.

Ghost

Ghost

He had no memory of flight.
No memory of time.
The silence in his world
was not his own choosing.
He could now see things
far away in the blackest
night.
The walls around him
were always white
but beyond his
touch.
He longed for the black
of nothing.
He longed for an end.

The Last Coming Storm

The Last Coming Storm

In the 'Middle Time',
indifference settled in like old dust
on a hot still day.
Shadows lay crisscrossed
in angry patterns
on the concreted ground,
reflecting the misconception
that grows like weeds,
giving only strength to the apathy
and borrowed fear

When there was nothing left to sell,
the 'Middle Time' withered
and died...
Without honour or ceremony.

Rusted metal and wire fences
have cut off
and replaced any remaining connection
we had
with History or green grass.

The Spider grinned his crooked grin
as he spun his web across the
abyss of man's greed, knowing
that he will eat well.
The only sound he hears
comes from behind
a crumbled wall.
Three[11] rats gnaw and snap away
on the carcass of a bird.

We still stand in groups
of three,
watching the pre-ordained prophets[12]
persecute the ideals
and promises
of freedom, history,
and choice.
We stand like vacant tourists
waiting for a bus
that will never come,
with no protection
from the falling yellow rain
that slowly erodes away our skin
and our resistance
to be who we really are.

There is a storm coming.
It will be the last one.
After it has past,
there will only be silence,
angry and cold...
For eternity.

The mind is like a spoiled child
constantly begging attention,
seeking the spot light.
While the body is denied
its separate identity
and forced into a life
of servitude
and loneliness.

Men Without Nations

Men
Without
Nations

Looking for the 'old days' gone,
sweet child, their smiles
a rainbow song.
Deserted from old dry river beds.
The spear they fear, no longer cries.

The weathered moon, promised in words,
of ancient men, lie forgotten
with their mortal fears,
are now masters of time.
They can be only heard as echoes
in a child's mind,
as laughter, food or rhyme.
But the jokes they tell
take flight, long to be free
from laughter, from opinions of trust.

They sleep unaware
of the Reptiles eyes of black glass,
that watch and wait
looking for an easy meal
of lust or hate.
They will eat well.

The Old Blind Bear
beyond the playground stands
on the stony ground, like a violin
strikes its mystic chords
beneath his feet.
While above his head
History floats
alone
above the dry river beds.

Their Society long ago complete,
they no longer use their dreams
to sleep
but shake apart the rational
dream
of Whirlwinds, Silence
and Snakes that speak.

The future, in a blind yellow rage,
yells out to the old Bear
to pretend
he can see
before the door closes on his cage.
But the Bear quietly speaks,
"I have the Key."

The new dawn,
promised long ago,
turned out to be nothing
but a gust of wind..
going the wrong way.

The
Time Circle

Alone, in the shadow of the time circle,
that is more mirror
then a doorway.
Lost on a winding path,
through a wilderness of time.

Alone, with no stopping place
or patience for the sick or dying.
On a pathway that is more chance
or secret dance
of memory...
A moving shadow
without a Master
to show the way.
against the ancient drama
of a constant state
of predawn.
The battlefield between night and day.

Here, in this unchanged
unchartered place,
I wander.
If I stop and listen,
I can hear the map makers
like beggars
at the back door...
Fumbling along like blind men,
looking for a (doorway) way in
through the wall of mist
that keeps me apart.

I can hear the rattling
of their iron keys
and the clattering of their
iron tongues.

I can smell their smoke
from their moldy fires

So I have chosen
not to sleep.

Alone, in the shadow of the Time Circle,
that is more true to the soul,
than real to the mind.
I stay lost in this windy dream.
watching the world
through the eyes
of a Bird.

The most humbling
and purest
experience one can have,
is to see the world
through the eyes
of a bird.

Addendum

1. History

History is a river of Time that records without judgement or prejudice, the passing parallel worlds that live side by side in the realities that make up and mark our living moment in Time. History, like the Earth, is a solitary traveler, who keeps much of what it knows secret and sacred. Until mankind learns not to only measure 'his relationship' to History but to embrace History's relationship to mankind then these secret visions will remain lost.

2. The Earth

The Earth is who we are, even though we spend so much time avoiding and denying this true reflection of reality of body and soul. The Earth is a vast lonely ship, slowly moving across the eternity of space and cold. Without anger or regret, she accepts her silent place among the vast sea of stars and tunnels of time. The Earth has only given of herself and man has only taken.

3. Clarity

Clarity is the free state of mind, body, spirit and shadow. It is excepting the preset boundaries of awareness that man is capable of grasping... and then going beyond. It is the dark face in the window that is tapping the glass to get your attention.

4. Bird

Each bird is like a silent prayer, dreaming for a chance to run alone and free. It is a true reflection of man' spirit. A mirror image of what we are capable of and what we ignore or have lost. Birds are a direct line to the parallel worlds that exist beyond our known boundaries. They are windows to these magically places for those who dare to take a peek.

5. Ghosts

A ghost is a spirit still connected to the energy of the physical Earth. It is without body or shadow or a sense of time and place. In some instances it clings desperately to an energy spot, not wanting to face the unknown, reflecting its fear and lack of awareness in its former bodied life. In other situations, the Earth herself will hold a Spirit, keeping it a prisoner until some problem is identified. Other spirits are just lost with nowhere to go. Lastly, death has just forgotten some ghosts.

6. Freedom

Freedom is the elusive wind, that plays games with our emotions and insecurities. It is our preordained right to spend our entire lives seeking it. To possess it. Even after death, freedom darts in and out among the trees, taunting us, wanting us to play. It is like the promise of a mountain of gold but once you have it, you have no way of carrying it home.

7. Duality

Duality is the ability to approach any idea, any gift or object with the clarity of both your personal response and that of a stranger. It is to understand that what is held out as 'truth' is not truth alone but also what is holding it out. What is up front and what is behind. Duality is also the ability to except the unknown as a mystery, choosing not to dissect it and expose it to situations beyond yours or its control. Duality is a given position on the wheel of life where chose is free to go either way.

8. Serpent

It is believed that our beginning as human beings started from the world ruled by Serpents. Strange beings (not snakes) from another world and another state of mind. They came and gave birth to not only our awareness as living entities on a living planet, but to our sense of history, thus creating a path to follow through time, to any given moment and beyond. They are still living among us though there numbers are few. They remain hidden in fear and dark places, in constant fear of man's growing numbers.

9. Civilization
The world can be measured in blocks of time when recording human activity across the vast expanse of History. Each block of time is referred to as a Civilization. We are now living in the fourth Civilization and true to the prophesies that prerecorded this human journey, we are at the very end of this 'time'. It was told that the end of this, the fourth civilization, would be heralded by worldwide environmental destruction and collapse. It was prophesied that man's intrusion and unwillingness to listen to the natural world will bring about the end (and hopefully the beginning of the fifth chance for a future).

10. Smoke
The early Serpents that ruled our world were masters of fire and discovered that fire created a fleeting chance to peek into other places in Time. Fire created smoke and this became a pathway to follow, like an arrow pointing the way. Our Spirits could be birds riding the warm winds of summer, to climb higher and higher. Smoke is a pathway with no end. It is a force that keeps in balance our shell of reality, our spirit, mind and body, and the unknown

11. Three
The number three represents the imbalance of clarity. It is dictated by aggression and confusion, promising long term results, while in reality surviving only for the moment. It is associated with greed and quick solutions. The 'even balance' of nature always starts with 'one' ending with two or visa versa. Three of anything

*foretells of hidden or pending danger and a misuse of
ones natural energy.*

12. **Prophet**
*An Ancient Priest or wise man/woman who perceives
and teaches the reality of life through the eyes of a bird
or animal or plant. They are true gypsies of the mind.
The road they wander is the River of Time. They belong
to no one race, free from any boundaries, physical or
political, They are not associated with any single family
or clan.*

Canadian Best Sellers
by Michael Robinson

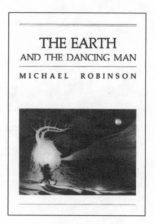

Other books by Michael Robinson are available at your local bookstore or can be ordered direct from the publisher.

The Earth and the Dancing Man $14.95
Touching the Serpent's Tail $14.95
A Bird within a Ring of Fire $14.95

ADD $3.00 postage and handling. Send cheque or money order.

Name. . . . .

Address. . . . .

City . . . . Postal Code . . . .

Martin House Publishing, R.R. 1, Keene, Ontario K0L 2G0 (705) 295-4491 Fax (705) 295-4124